2021

Treasured Poets

Edited By Jenni Harrison

First published in Great Britain in 2021 by:

Young Writers
Remus House
Coltsfoot Drive
Peterborough
PE2 9BF
Telephone: 01733 890066
Website: www.youngwriters.co.uk

All Rights Reserved
Book Design by Ashley Janson
© Copyright Contributors 2021
Softback ISBN 978-1-80015-502-2

Printed and bound in the UK by BookPrintingUK
Website: www.bookprintinguk.com
YB0476I

FOREWORD

Welcome Reader!

Are you ready to discover weird and wonderful creatures that you'd never even dreamed of?

For Young Writers' latest competition we asked primary school pupils to create a Peculiar Pet of their own invention, and then write a poem about it! They rose to the challenge magnificently and the result is this fantastic collection full of creepy critters and amazing animals!

Here at Young Writers our aim is to encourage creativity in children and to inspire a love of the written word, so it's great to get such an amazing response, with some absolutely fantastic poems. Not only have these young authors created imaginative and inventive animals, they've also crafted wonderful poems to showcase their creations and their writing ability. These poems are brimming with inspiration. The slimiest slitherers, the creepiest crawlers and furriest friends are all brought to life in these pages – you can decide for yourself which ones you'd like as a pet!

I'd like to congratulate all the young authors in this anthology, I hope this inspires them to continue with their creative writing.

★ CONTENTS ★

Hockley Primary School, Hockley

Caleb Penson (11)	1
Beth I (11)	2
Auré Coidan (11)	4
Albie R (10)	5
Sophie H (11)	6
Austin D (10)	8
Evie J (11)	10
Fletcher C (11)	11
Olivia Wareham (10)	12
Molly Solesbury (10)	14
Eva Marek (10)	15
Kaitlin B (11)	16
Zac S (10)	17
Matthew N (10)	18
Olivia Mcdougall (10)	19
Isla W (10)	20
Charlotte D (10)	21
Harry D (10)	22
Aiden A-C (11)	23
Esmee Blackwell (11)	24
Rowan Gray (10)	25
Elijah Turner (10)	26
Arjun Ayyappan (10)	27
Madalena Pires (10)	28
William Eaton (11)	29
Oliver W (10)	30
Jacob W (10)	31
Malcolm Gray (8)	32
Freya J (10)	33
Luke I (9)	34
Billy O (11)	35
Dylan Emmanuel (11)	36
Alexander Doherty (9)	37
Maisie D (10)	38
Caleb K (11)	39
Sophia McCormack-King (10)	40
Clara W (9)	41
Elise S (11)	42
Caitlin G (10)	43
Issy-May Barham (11)	44
Archer Ford (10)	45
Lorenzo Malanga (9)	46

Holway Park Community Primary School, Taunton

Scott Cridlin (11)	47
Ben Kidner (11)	48
Corey Deverill (11)	50
Sonny Foreman (11)	52
Destiny McGuinness (11)	54
Harry Parsons (11)	56
Rosie Skinner (10)	57
Kieran Denness (11)	58
Poppy Lowe (10)	60
Cherokie-Rose Scanes (11)	61
Ellie-May Harvey (10)	62
George Cook (11)	63
Calvin Livesey (11)	64
Sadie Greedy (10)	65
Charlie Lawson (11)	66
Kenzie Roe (11)	67
Lily Lang (11)	68
Harvey Livesey (11)	69
Chloe Stacey (10)	70
Maddi Barber (10)	71
Scarlett Clapp (11)	72
Jacob Closs (11)	73
Marina Rutherford (11)	74
Robert McLean (10)	75

Harry Haddon (11)	76
Ashton Curtis (11)	77
Zoe Stacey (10)	78
Imogen Grant (10)	79
Leah Banthorpe (11)	80

Palterton Primary School, Palterton

Millie Marsden (10)	81
Esmae Irons (9)	82
Angel Asher (11)	84
Jacob Smith (11)	86
Enis Kayran (11)	87
Niamh Gotteri (10)	88
Darcie Bailey (9)	90
Ted Grainger-Grimes (10)	91
Sophie Ford (9)	92
Harry Carr (11)	93
Max Slater (11)	94
Jacob Galley (11)	95
Taylor Kirby (11)	96
Paige Darby (10)	97
Troy Everitt (10)	98
Amelia Wombwell (10)	99
Dacey Harris (9)	100
Archie Clayton (11)	101
Barney Clayton (7)	102
Jensen Wombwell (10)	103

Parkinson Lane Community Primary School, Halifax

Hiba Junaid (10)	104
Aamnah Javed (10)	105
Aleena Ali (10)	106

Turners Hill CE Primary School, Turners Hill

Lola Rykala (8)	107
Isabelle Violet Staples (8)	108
Jessica Thrower (7)	109
Oliver Thrower (7)	110

Weston Junior Academy, Weston Coyney

Jessica Botham (8)	111
Leon Scholtz (10)	112
Jasmine Dawkins (10)	113

Winterbourne Boys' Academy, Thornton Heath

Angel Reid-Holden (11)	114
Raza Khan (11)	115
Dhyan Patel (9)	116
Richard Agyei Opoku (10)	117
Nathaniel Suthaskumar (10)	118
Hamed Jimoh (11)	119
Reuben Oviawe (7)	120

THE POEMS

Michael Monkey

M ichael Monkey is the best artist in the world like 100 Leonardo Da Vincis
I ntelligent Michael makes sure no one finds out who he is
C olourful pictures that he makes, the more pictures people want to take
H is signature is very unique as it is a lightning bolt and it's like a real one
A s much of an amazing monkey he is, he could get found out at some point
E verybody loves his art and they want to see much more
L ovely Michael has very pointy toes and he has his own T-shirt and hat

M agnificent little monkey he is and what a great artist he is
O ne picture that he makes is amazing and great
N othing can get in his way
K een, adventurous and sneaky too
E ntertaining people with his art
Y ou need to watch out, you don't know when there's a monkey about.

Caleb Penson (11)
Hockley Primary School, Hockley

Coco The Gymnastics Crazy Guinea Pig

Coco the guinea pig,
Very, very bendy,
Really not big,
Her leotards are trendy.

She soars through the sky,
Crowds cheer loudly,
People wave as she passes by,
Fellow guinea pigs watch proudly.

Her name is Coco,
She's performed around the world,
London, America and Tokyo,
Where she's leapt and twirled.

When on the bar,
She does her best,
Coco's in the lead by far,
She shuffles to the east,
Then to the west.

Flipping like crazy,
She twists around,
She's nowhere near lazy,
For gymnastics is what she found.

Swinging higher and higher,
Coco gets ready,
She looks like a flyer,
She lands very steady.

  C razy,
  O utstanding,
  C ool,
  O h, wow!

Beth I (11)
Hockley Primary School, Hockley

The Origin Of Muscle Monkey

Timmy the monkey went walking one day,
Off he went walking to his best friend's house in May.
When he tripped on a hill halfway through the town,
All of a sudden he began to roll down.
He rolled on for miles, all the way to the big city,
Then stopped and came face-to-face with a kitty
They fought for an hour, for no reason at all
Then Timmy wished for help, with nobody to call.
Just then came a cloud, and another, and more,
They all came together at 5 past 4.
Then came the thunder and then came the lightning,
The kitty ran away, too scared to be fighting.
Then, disaster happened, Timmy was struck!
He got blown away to on top of a truck.
Then when he woke up, Timmy felt hungry
Hungry to stop crime, because he was now...
Muscle Monkey!

Auré Coidan (11)
Hockley Primary School, Hockley

My Best Friend

It has big green eyes and flaming red hair on its head,
And he lurks at the very bottom of my bed.
His body is covered in golden scales as bright as the sun,
He hides in cupboards and jumps out at Mum.
At night his snuffling, snarly, fiery nose,
Breathes warm air on my little frozen toes.
As he snores he lets out a strange screeching sound,
That scares birds out of the sky from miles around.
He has a huge tummy and needs lots of meat,
I steal it from the table and drop it by my feet.
His name is Michael and he's my very best friend,
I know we will be together till the very end.
Because he loves climbing, jumping and making strange smells too,
And because he knows that friendship based on love is always the most true.

Albie R (10)
Hockley Primary School, Hockley

Lottie My Guineadoggy

Sometimes when I want to play
Lottie my guineadoggy saves the day
With dark brown fur
And she doesn't purr
Lottie and I
Have an amazing time
She wears a bow
I wear a tie
Then we eat our favourite, apple pie
But Lottie isn't like a dog or a cat
She doesn't like to pee on the mat
Lottie is, well, very peculiar
And all my friends want to play with her
But if she is seen
She'll have to sail overseas.

And live in a zoo
Surrounded by monkey poo
Lottie is very clever
You would know if you got to meet her
She lives in a cage on my bedroom floor
On the left-hand side near my door.

Today was a good day
And the time flew by
But Lottie and I
Have to say goodbye.

Sophie H (11)
Hockley Primary School, Hockley

Doctor L Bug

Doctor L Bug
Is very peculiar
He loves the band
The Lazy Loopiars

He specialises
In three different things
Medicine, X-rays
But mostly stings

He has eight legs
He has eight arms
He has a huge tongue
He means no harm

Doctor L Bug
Has three horns
He goes to Narnia
To talk to the fawns

He lives next to work
Down Beetle Drive

His favourite dip
Is sour cream and chive

He likes eating grass
He snacks on leaves
He loves playing football
With his best friend Steve

Doctor L Bug
Likes making new friends
He wants to keep them
Till the world ends.

Austin D (10)
Hockley Primary School, Hockley

Cleo The Caterpillar

Cleo the caterpillar lived on a hill
She liked to look at flowers at the bottom of her hill
She went to see her friends Bubbly Bob and Squiggle Wiggle
But she was feeling very ill
So she visited a doctorpillar
He said, "Oh, you have a common colderpillar."
Cleo bought some chocopillars to make her feel better
Once she got home she saw a big bowerpillar
She walked inside and saw a caterpillar picture
With her friends Bubbly Bob and Squiggle Wiggle
She felt a lot betterpillar so they played but that's not the end
Cleo fell down the hillerpillar
And woke up in her comfy bederpillar
She said "Argh! Oh, it was a dreamerpillar."

Evie J (11)
Hockley Primary School, Hockley

Poppy And Nala The Super Pets

Poppy is a dummy
Although she is very funny
She eats a lot of Bakers
Although she does like crackers

Nala goes *stomp, stomp, stomp*, just like a king
Even though she does like to swing
Nala will get through all her toys
Yet today she isn't even one

Poppy sadly passed away in 2020
She was thirteen and had a very good life
Now she is up in Heaven with all the tennis balls
She always tried to lick dinner off the big knife

Nala is obsessed with cheese
Her favourite place to be is the 200ft garden
She likes my dad's car, even when she gets sick
Nala is a hardened-up dog.

Fletcher C (11)
Hockley Primary School, Hockley

Wagon The Dragon Goes On A Trip!

Wagon the dragon was a kind and friendly dragon
He was alone and sad again
"I want to go on a trip again!"
The first time ever
He'd better check the weather
He hopped on his wagon
This very friendly dragon
It started pouring
Then it started roaring
He didn't care
He needed some fresh air
His fox tail was leaving a rather long trail
He was getting weary
He had some sweeties
Wagon the dragon was sitting on his wagon
"I don't like the trip," said the dragon
He was out in the wild
"Please I'm only a child!"

He made his way back home
All alone...

Olivia Wareham (10)
Hockley Primary School, Hockley

Different Dolphin

D ifferent Dolphin as extraordinary as can be
I s ready and prepared
F or the next adventure to arrive
F un is what he is
E very day means smiling all the time
R eady for adventure after adventure
E ven when he is unwell
N ever giving up
T rying everything

D aring to do anything
O n the lookout for messy people (just like himself)
L ife means so much which...
P uts him in an extremely jolly mood
H eidi is his best friend
I nside his life he will
N ever lose his happiness!

Molly Solesbury (10)
Hockley Primary School, Hockley

Steve The Sloth

S teve the sloth is very peculiar
T he fastest living thing on Earth
E ven faster than lightning
V ery strange, really weird
E verything that gets in his way, he will run through

T he funniest thing in the world
H is light green hair blowing behind him as he runs
E ven though he is a sloth he can beat Usain Bolt

S teve is my sloth
L augh all day
O pen your eyes and see him race through town
T onight he's going to make the crowd go, "Wow!"
H e's the best sloth in the world!

Eva Marek (10)
Hockley Primary School, Hockley

Anthony The Ant

Anthony the ant is a big ant
As big as big can be
He is not a saint, not a jolly old mate
No, this is not Anthony.
He stomps on his foes and licks their toes
Then eats their bones
Now this is Anthony!
One day Anthony was stuffed into a jar, sad and unhappy
Then, his owner made a mistake
To take out Anthony
Now the ant wanted revenge
So licked his head and toes
Then tasted his nose
What a good one, what a good catch!
So Anthony gobbled him whole!
Anthony is lonely, Anthony is sad
Well, at least Dad didn't taste too bad.

Kaitlin B (11)
Hockley Primary School, Hockley

Lash Rider

L ovely dog that will comfort you and make you feel better
A mazingly controls lightning as his superpower
S carily, when he gets angry he glows up with lightning
H appily, he runs around every day having a great time

R unning around to charge up his lightning
I nk is his weakness as it de-strengthens him
D upla is his best friend as he plays with him every day
E veryone thinks he is different
R ider, the part of Lash Rider, is for when he goes too fast he rides things.

Zac S (10)
Hockley Primary School, Hockley

My Great Pet, Snaker

My peculiar, interesting, scaled pet is a pet like no other.
He has eight legs and saves people who are in trouble.
He can do anything...
Fly like Superman, shrink tiny like Ant-Man,
Shape-shift, go invisible, walk through fire,
Breathe underwater and spit out webs.
My gentle pet is not here to hurt you,
He is here to help you.
He lives in his little bunker
With a tiny TV and tiny toilet.
He likes flying around in the fresh air
Like a bird or a plane.
He knows when you need help, so don't worry.

Matthew N (10)
Hockley Primary School, Hockley

Wizard Bee

W ith all of her strength she finally defeated the bad guy
I t was a really hard fight and now she's so tired
Z oom! She went back to her beehive
A s she went in her house her family and friends surprised her with a party
R elieved with excitement she hugged all her family and friends
D on't mess with Wizard Bee because she is the strongest bee ever

B ees are brilliant and amazing
E very day Wizard Bee fights with bad guys
E very time she wins.

Olivia Mcdougall (10)
Hockley Primary School, Hockley

Doctor, Doctor

I have a little pet,
No, he is not a vet.

He may look big and strong
But he has wanted to be a doctor all along

"Woof!" is what he says when he isn't sure
But he'll always be around when you need a paw.

He tends to his patients each and every day
Not caring about how much his boss will pay

My dog, he'll try his hardest
He'll do all the problems which are the largest.

This is why he deserves some praise
Because every day my dog's life is a maze.

Isla W (10)
Hockley Primary School, Hockley

Petrica The Paligator

Petricia the paligator
Has a marvellous horn
She was the type of alligator
Who liked being drawn
Her teeth were sharp and bloody
Which was very gory
I was her pen pal buddy
At least no more
One day she left me
No longer afraid
She was drinking tea you see
No longer in the shade
My heart was a tail
Very rough
I found one of her scales
Which was very tough
I never saw her again
Even though I tried
I used her pen
To keep her spirit alive.

Charlotte D (10)
Hockley Primary School, Hockley

Party Unicorn Dog

The dog that flies goes down the stream
And ends up in the ocean ring
He flies over to an island that no one can see
He's gone to bed and has a dream
A fish comes along and says, "Feed me!"
He has no food, not even for him
Is he going to starve?
What's happening?
Then he wakes and sees the fish,
He has some food and they both get what they wish.
They dine together and eat all night
Till the sun comes up all nice and bright!

Harry D (10)
Hockley Primary School, Hockley

Pawing Holly

Miaow! Holly was turning into a grumpy, lazy cat
Just then she scratched me
But her cute stare emptied my mind
I forgot why I was mad

I stroked her furry head and she put her paw on mine
I suddenly had flashbacks thrown at me
Whoosh! Bang! They went inside my gigantic head

It felt like she was telling me
That she found a way to communicate with me
Miaow! came a muffled sound
Turning into human words!

Aiden A-C (11)
Hockley Primary School, Hockley

Here Comes Burrito

Burrito comes to steal your food,
Sorry, he doesn't mean to be rude,
He looks at you with those puppy-dog eyes,
If you refuse to play, he cries,
But the biggest game of all,
Is not fetch the ball,
Instead it's called 'be a cannibal',
Don't worry though, it's not that bad,
It's not completely crazy mad,
The thing that he eats isn't flesh and blood though...

It's none other than a burrito!

Esmee Blackwell (11)
Hockley Primary School, Hockley

Savage Stan

S uper evil in all ways is something he is
A dvanced Dog is his arch-enemy
V ector Von Cat is his first-hand man
A nnihilating the villain competition is his goal
G nats are what his army of
E vil henchmen is made from.

S tan has huge fangs
T he superpowers he has are intelligence and fire hands
A nd Stan's weakness is catbrainiem
N ever ever gives up in battle.

Rowan Gray (10)
Hockley Primary School, Hockley

Bowie Jr The Musical Titanaboa

Bowie is a very fun, amazing snake
He wakes up every morning
And tunes his sound strings to make them perfect
Ping! Pong! Pong! he goes
He would slither to me so I can give him his food
Which is sushi, his most-loved food
I come to him while he eats
To stroke his Costa Rican viridescent skin
Next he plays his instruments
Which is some of his best, most alluring features he has
He is very crucial to me and I love him.

Elijah Turner (10)
Hockley Primary School, Hockley

Gigantic Gizmo Got The Goal!

Gigantic Gizmo got the goal
Even though he felt like he'd lost his soul
Unfortunately during the match he fell in a hole
He rolled and rolled and rolled
Gizmo saw a mole
Who told him to stop to roll
He told him to get up and stop being a baby
Gizmo went back to the pitch, full of rage and anger
That the minuscule mole called him a baby
Suddenly he scored the goal
And got the award of being gorilla of the match.

Arjun Ayyappan (10)
Hockley Primary School, Hockley

My Balloon Dog

Squeex is my dog, my peculiar balloon dog
He's very unique, I can tell you that
Instead of barking he squeaks like a rat
He jumps in the air like he just doesn't care

Squeex is my dog, my playful balloon dog.
He jumps, he rolls, he just has fun
He chases butterflies as they fly in the sun
But he just doesn't like it when the fun is done

Squeex may not be ordinary, but he is extraordinary.

Madalena Pires (10)
Hockley Primary School, Hockley

The Dog Poem

My dog barks, barks like a fox.
The dog is small, small like a baby crocodile.
The dog is cute, cuter than a mouse.
The dog is five years old.
Like any other dog, he likes to go out for a walk.
Like any other cute dog, he has a lead and collar
To stop him running away and chasing other dogs.
He is beautiful like every dog.
He is also loud like a lion screaming.
He is tiny like a little squirrel.

William Eaton (11)
Hockley Primary School, Hockley

Lazy Liam

Lazy Liam
Never went to school
He would stay at home
And pretend to be cool
Playing with his mates
He would always have fun
Going to bed at 1!

Lazy Liam is very bright
His colour shines in the night
Shooting rainbows in the air
Girls come from everywhere!

Lazy Liam is very lazy
Not as much fun
But he's not as lazy
As his best friend Max!

Oliver W (10)
Hockley Primary School, Hockley

Phoenix The Flyer

Phoenix the horse and I were ready for adventure
We waited for night to take flight
In the air I realised the moon was very bright
Zooming through the sky so fast I thought I'd die
Then I looked at his fur, it was as dark as bark
It was time to stop then *pop!*
Before we knew it, it was sunrise
We descended down to the ground
And I thought, *what a night!*

Jacob W (10)
Hockley Primary School, Hockley

Super Dog

S uper Dog is the smartest dog in the world, breaking laws every day
U p, up and away Super Dog goes
P erfect clean paws and shiny silver fur
E ats green vegetables all day long
R an the marathon thirty seconds sharp

D ogs fear Super Dog in dark midnight
O ut of the house into the sky
G one to save people in the night.

Malcolm Gray (8)
Hockley Primary School, Hockley

Rainbow Riley The Rainbow Chipmunk

Rainbow Riley!

Rainbow Riley, did you hear?
Zoom! Zoom! Zoom! Around it's clear
She's bright, she's colourful, furry too
She's incredible and clever, who knew?

Rainbow Riley oh so fast
In a race she's never last
She's never been seen running around
Rainbow Riley, you scorch the ground!

Rainbow Riley.

Freya J (10)
Hockley Primary School, Hockley

Chipster The Guinea Pig

C hipster prefers being called Chip
H arm her, and she'll give you a nip
I n her cage it looks like a gym
P ut her in the bath and she'll swim, swim, swim!
S he can easily outrun a rat
T hrough the woods do the same with a bat
E very day, we will go on a run
R acing away, we have lots of fun!

Luke I (9)
Hockley Primary School, Hockley

The Dogocorn

D angerous Dogocorn rummaging through the bag of rubbish
O nly the Dogocorn has spots like this
G iant dog barking at the tall Dogocorn
O h! He's starting to fly! Into the moonlight
C orn is his favourite food
O nce he comes back down to Earth
R un, Dogocorn!
N o pet is quite like it.

Billy O (11)
Hockley Primary School, Hockley

DJ Chiggy

Chiggy is like a mini boulder
He sits and raps on my shoulder
He's the most amazing pet
I remember when we met
I was walking alone, and I found this bone
So I kept it, 'cause it looked like chicken
But, just then a chick started pecking
I thought to call him Ziggy
But I thought of a better name...
That was DJ Chiggy.

Dylan Emmanuel (11)
Hockley Primary School, Hockley

Donald The Floating Duck

Donald the floating duck
He will help anyone when they are stuck
Everyone will be frightened
Donald is tightened
Until he lets all the air out

Everyone is scared to look
Apart from Donald's owner, Mr Cook
"Isn't this amazing?" said the shopkeeper May
Once again, he's saved the day!

Alexander Doherty (9)
Hockley Primary School, Hockley

Pal And Me

Pal and me went on a ride
Voosh through the blue sky
We saw bikes fly by
Pal dropped, I think he was a bit sick!
Pal got sad, we went to see a crab
Crab snapped, Pal was glad again
Wow! What a busy day for a penguin pal
My little penguin helped me on his back
And *voosh!* We went back.

Maisie D (10)
Hockley Primary School, Hockley

Loyal Doggostein

D on't underestimate Doggostein
O rders you give he will do
G o get shopping
G o get mopping
O nly for you
S o don't underestimate Doggostein
T o make you happy
E very day, every night
I n order to make you feel
N aughty.

Caleb K (11)
Hockley Primary School, Hockley

Laila The Octopus

Laila the octopus
Was feeling rather illopus
She went to the doctopus
The doctopus said, "You've got a symptom of spotopus!"
She bought some sockopus so that
She can cover her spotopus
Then she felt betteropus
She took her sockopus off
And went to play with Olly the octopus.

Sophia McCormack-King (10)
Hockley Primary School, Hockley

Super Poppy

Poppy is a super dog
Poppy can move electricity
So when a bad guy is around
She takes to the sky and hits the ground.
She needs to practise her flying though
When there is a bad bang she is on the go.
She keeps her flying a secret
We have the best times
Me and my super dog.

Clara W (9)
Hockley Primary School, Hockley

Muffy R

M arvellous
U nique
F luffy
F antastic
Y outhful

Muffy is fluffy,
Has known to be naughty
Wears a baseball hat and funky shades
Reads at night
Sleeps all day
Eats every hour of his day
What a peculiar pet.

Elise S (11)
Hockley Primary School, Hockley

My Black And White Cat

Gentle and smooth just like her name
Cute but messy just like me
She was a normal cat
Who liked to play
Until she saw a bird in place
She was a clever little thing
But hides from you
Yesterday she had anger in her eyes.

Caitlin G (10)
Hockley Primary School, Hockley

Fashion Koala

As fashionable as a model and really creative as an artist
Always doing fashion like making her own dress
As colourful as the rainbow
As clever as a human
As nice as a flower
As brave as a lion
As old as pieces of wood.

Issy-May Barham (11)
Hockley Primary School, Hockley

Lurking Labrador Goes For A Stroll

One day Lurking Labrador
Decided that he would walk some more
So he got up on his skinny legs
Went to his human, and started to beg
The human let him go for a stroll
Little did the human know he went to the mall.

Archer Ford (10)
Hockley Primary School, Hockley

Slow Snail

Slow as a bike
But I'm still a snail
I can climb to your rooftops
And reach the leaves in the tallest trees
Insects avoid my sticky trail
But I will always be a slow snail.

Lorenzo Malanga (9)
Hockley Primary School, Hockley

Samuel's Life

There once is a froggy who roams the land,
His name is Samuel, the kind friendly frog,
Samuel dislikes the sad, sandy sand,
But loves playing on a lovely log.

Samuel loves hopping around the park,
Can't be stopped, he's as fast as a dart,
When night will come, the dogs will bark,
When it's fighting, he won't be torn apart.

Samuel is just a cute little frog, yes!
Oh, he's just so cute, oh he's just so cute,
Just adorable, never in a mess,
Now he goes to see his friend, Mr Newt.

They talk for a time, they become best friends,
And that's the end.

Scott Cridlin (11)
Holway Park Community Primary School, Taunton

Colin The Catnarie And His Peculiar Friends

A lpacas are animals and are all amazing.
B ees and bugs are always buzzing and are busy.
C olin the catnarie kicks and clicks.
D inosaurs were dead decillion decades ago.
E lephants have trunks that entrench and entwine.
F ishies love to flop, flap and flurry.
G oats gulp down gates, even ghosts.
H orses can help honeymooners get happy.
I guanas give instructions to intoxicate or intimidate.
J ellyfish jump and jiggle about.
K angaroos fly kites and take lots of kips.
L adybirds lavish in lady-like lotions.
M ongooses microwave microscopic milk.
N arwhals navigate nasty nuggets.
O ctopuses obtain obese orators.
P iranhas pick up lots of pelicans.
Q ueens are kinda animals as they're qualified quits.

R hinos are radical and eat red meat.
S loths salute to salad and salami.
T urtles like to transmit tomatoes.
U nicorns usher to urinate.
V ipers hate the vets because they violate.
W alruses writhe and watch the waves.
X enomorph is xeroxed and x-rayed as he's an alien.
Y aks yank yeast and make yoghurt.
Z ebras zap and zigzag zuchinis.

Ben Kidner (11)
Holway Park Community Primary School, Taunton

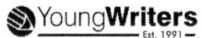

Percy The Penguin's Acrobatic Rap!

A crobatic, active, ambitious
B rilliant, bashful
C ool, crazy creature
D aring, determined daredevil
E fficient, energetic, excited
F abulous, friendly, fearless
G reat, giddy, grateful
H appy, hilarious, helpful
I ndependent, intelligent
J oker, jolly
K ind, knowledgable
L ittle lazy
M enacingly marvellous, mysterious
N oble, noisy, nervous
O utstanding, obedient
P erfect Percy Penguin
Q uiet
R ad, reliable, reluctant
S illy, small, salty

T ruthful, thoughtful
U nbelievable, unbeaten
V igilant, victorious
W eary, willing
X enophobic
Y oung
Z ooming, zany.

Corey Deverill (11)
Holway Park Community Primary School, Taunton

Pub Bodyboard Pat Portable

Here is Pat Portable,
Stop, slow down and speed up time he is able,
Pat Portable is teleportable,
In his chubby lips
He uses his teeth to eat chips,
Having infinite darts,
He hates farts,
With his antennae of time
And his turkey legs to stop crime.

Here is Pat Portable,
Stop, slow down and speed up time he is able,
Pat Portable is teleportable,
With his witty brain
And humour he accidentally brings pain,
Using his gargantuan eyes,
He sees some guys,
They're trying to break in,
So he freezes time and puts them in a bin.

Here is Pat Portable,
Stop, slow down and speed up time he is able,
Pat Portable is teleportable,
Bang! Crash! They're now dead,
While their wives are lying in bed.

Sonny Foreman (11)
Holway Park Community Primary School, Taunton

Ninja Frog The Strange Hero

You could see him in your neighbourhood
Or sometimes in the woods.

Ninja Frog's eyes are so big and wide
And he dashes through the air with a glide.

If he's sitting on a log
And smells like a bog
Of course, it's Ninja Frog!

He is the bravest frog in town
And never has a frown.

Although his mask is a bin bag
He is still able to zigzag.

If he is sitting on a log
And smells like a bog
Of course, it's Ninja Frog!

His skin is so slimy
And also very shiny.

He is our hero
You will never see him slow.

Even though it's the end
Just remember our fellow friend!

Destiny McGuinness (11)
Holway Park Community Primary School, Taunton

The Brilliant Mr Bippo

The brilliant one and only hero
Who is the speed of light, *zoom, zoom, zoom!*
The one and only great Mr Bippo
Under the earth he goes, *boom, boom, boom!*

Fighting big bad bosses, blinding the bully
After that he went back to sweet, sweet home
Then a man came in wearing a hoodie
Suddenly a bag came over his dome.

He went with the man under the cover
But Mr Bippo had a plan in his bag
He pretended to be the man's brother
He zoomed out quickly in a zigzag.

Suddenly, well, he snuck out at the back
Then he plopped on his good trusty hat.

Harry Parsons (11)
Holway Park Community Primary School, Taunton

Tilly The Turkey

This is Tilly the turkey
He is a little bit quirky
Tilly likes steak pie
And he's a little sly
His feathers are pink and green
They're the most beautiful you have seen.

He has bright orange feet
With a beaming yellow beak
His hat is as dark as the night
Tilly has no fright
His wings spread wide
And he began to glide
Terrific Tilly goes *bang, boom, baa!*

Rosie Skinner (10)
Holway Park Community Primary School, Taunton

What Am I?

When I'm mute
I am cute
I am clean
I lean
Not very often
I don't like cuddles
I cause a lot of troubles
I'm mixed
I'm a furry friend...
I'm kind of mischievous
I'm kind of mysterious
I like cheese
I like it breezy
I hate cats
I'm not a fan of them
I'm a pet you could own...
What am I?
50% chinchilla, 50% rat
I'm majestic
I'm very clean and cute

I will clean for you
I will protect you
I'm better at protection.

Kieran Denness (11)
Holway Park Community Primary School, Taunton

The Silly Syena

This is a syena
It is half hyena
The other half is a seal
It loves a nice warm meal
You think it is crazy
But it is really lazy
If you enter his property
You won't win the lottery
He will play
Every day
Then will go for a nap
And collect some sap
This is one of a kind
It's different in your mind
This animal is strange
But it should never change.

Poppy Lowe (10)
Holway Park Community Primary School, Taunton

Vulpix The Nine-Tailed Wolf

V ulpix the nine-tailed magic wolf has
U ndiscovered powers like
L aser eyes
P aralysation
I ndependence
X -ray vision

T eleportation
H ealing
E ndangered

W ater
O ver-protectiveness
L uminous is the end of her tail
F luffy is how she feels.

Cherokie-Rose Scanes (11)
Holway Park Community Primary School, Taunton

Doggy Disco

Nunpty is clumsy
His favourite drink is a pupichino
And he's also a very big weirdo.
When he's sad he goes really mad.
He can sing like a human
And he dances like a headless chicken.
He plays with a ball
But he also drools.
Nunpty is wet
But he also sweats.
He is the best dog you have ever met!

Ellie-May Harvey (10)
Holway Park Community Primary School, Taunton

Meet Morpho Norto

Morpho is cool
But you always have to check your pool
He can bite
And has threatening fights.

Morpho can dance
And super prance
He can swim
With evil Harlequin.

He can camouflage
And super sabotage
If you touch his property
You will get a 0.001% chance of winning the lottery.

George Cook (11)
Holway Park Community Primary School, Taunton

The Acrostic Kosloth

K osloth is my perfect peculiar pet.
O kay, Kosloth is clever and cute.
S o share my perfect, peculiar pet.
L et him play his great guitar.
O h, by the way, he's a guitarist.
T ell people about my peculiar, perfect pet.
H e will be a very happy Kosloth.

Calvin Livesey (11)
Holway Park Community Primary School, Taunton

The Super Slophin

Slophins are funny,
When you tickle their tummy.
They swim all day long,
While singing a song.
They go for a nap
And get a tap.
Maybe a new friend,
A hand he might lend.
I'll give him a tour,
To swim some more.
Now that's the end,
So goodbye my friend.

Sadie Greedy (10)
Holway Park Community Primary School, Taunton

Slakephant

S plash!
L ives in a swamp
A nd I'm in a big grump
K ids run away
E very day
P lay with water
H ave fun with my daughter
A nd I hope I never see ya
N either do I care
T hank you for listening!

Charlie Lawson (11)
Holway Park Community Primary School, Taunton

Funny Bunny

I'm funny
But only when it's sunny
I am really peculiar
Every day in October
Because if not it hurts my tummy.

I'm a sneaky puppy
But not very fluffy
But I try to think
But it comes out with a blink
But you can call me yucky.

Kenzie Roe (11)
Holway Park Community Primary School, Taunton

Tabby The Cat

T ail
A dorable
B eautiful
B amboo loving
Y oung

T ame
H appy
E dgy

C ute
A nxious
T oasty

Tabby is my BFF.

Lily Lang (11)
Holway Park Community Primary School, Taunton

Seaguin

S liding down the ice
E very day it hunts
A nd it has huge wings
G oing shopping, run!
U nder the snow, gliding about
I n the Antarctic
N o, it is not friendly!

Harvey Livesey (11)
Holway Park Community Primary School, Taunton

Perfect, Peculiar Poppy

I like playing with snow.
I make people go, "Woah!"
I have black and white fur.
I usually like to purr.
I am a tricky mix.
What am I?

I am a mix between a polar bear and cow.

Chloe Stacey (10)
Holway Park Community Primary School, Taunton

Percy Pig

My name is Percy Pig
I have a kind buddy called Tig
I adore rolling in mud
I sometimes think of blood
My owner is quite big
It's okay, they love me, their lil' pig.

Maddi Barber (10)
Holway Park Community Primary School, Taunton

The Pigaka

P eople stare at Pigaka as
I nnocent as she is.
G ory but glamorous
A nd amazingly unique.
K ind but deadly if woken
A nd awfully crazy.

Scarlett Clapp (11)
Holway Park Community Primary School, Taunton

Wolf Of The Demi-Gods, Afmel

- **A** mazing, athletic, acrobatic
- **F** ast, furious, friendly
- **M** ean, malicious, metal
- **E** legant, enthusiastic, energetic
- **L** ovely, likeable, liveable.

Jacob Closs (11)
Holway Park Community Primary School, Taunton

Sid The Sloth

My name is Sid
And I am just a kid
I'm extraordinary and rare
Just like a Care Bear
I can be silly
But so is my friend, Billy
My name is Sid the sloth.

Marina Rutherford (11)
Holway Park Community Primary School, Taunton

Out Of This World

Such an outer space-like creature
As long as many o' metre
It's dangerous enough
And so very tough
You probably won't want to meet her!

Robert McLean (10)
Holway Park Community Primary School, Taunton

The Worm

There once was a worm from Taunton
Who always ate all the Thorntons
He got so fat
He sat on the cat
And he always went to Braunton.

Harry Haddon (11)
Holway Park Community Primary School, Taunton

Silly Sid

Once in the tree there was a sloth
Who was always as dry as a cloth
Up the tree
The sloth he should be
And be as still as a moth.

Ashton Curtis (11)
Holway Park Community Primary School, Taunton

Llama Life

Llama is often in lots of drama
And always lots of karma
She is a star
On Saturday she goes to the bar
And hides from the farmer.

Zoe Stacey (10)
Holway Park Community Primary School, Taunton

A Groovy Welcoming

My name is Hannah,
I work in a manor,
I'm hard to find,
Although I'm very kind.
My name is Hannah the hammerhead!

Imogen Grant (10)
Holway Park Community Primary School, Taunton

The Dogadile

I'm a dogadile
Not a crocodile
Not a dog
I like to sit on the bog
On the tiles
I'm a dogadile.

Leah Banthorpe (11)
Holway Park Community Primary School, Taunton

My Dancing Doggy

Introducing my dancing doggy, Bruce,
By the end of this you will know him crazily.
We brought him from Leeds when he was a pup.
When we had him we knew he was rough.
We took him to the vets and he had a lump on his back.
After the vets we brought him back,
He made a friend, his name is Jack.
He sat on the sofa knowing that he was home
But he knew that he was going to be alone.
He wiggled and jiggled all around
And my mum thought he was crazy and cute,
She thought he was dancing but he was prancing.
Now he is four he's such a good pet to adore,
That's the loved half of him
But on the other side he is very cheeky.
He will go around the garden for thirty minutes
With socks, tights, clothing, shoes and stockings.
Now you know him crazily well
And that's my dancing doggy.

Millie Marsden (10)
Palterton Primary School, Palterton

My Dancing Uni-Pug

Introducing my pooch, Pepper-Belle
By the end of this poem you will know her well.
We rescued her from a broken home,
Desperate to stop her being all alone.
Pepper 'part pug' is her breed,
We bought her a new collar and lead.
Queen of Huggles is her nickname,
Hugging is how she got her fame.
Snuggling and fussing became her job role,
Working for a therapy dog charity, their hearts she stole.
Visiting residents poorly in their hospital beds,
Love, hugs, warmth and happiness she spreads.
Walking in the rain she absolutely hates,
Though in the sunshine she thinks it's great.
Super-speed zoomies happen every day,
"100mph Doggy - quick get out of her way!"
Crunchy carrots and apple are her healthy treats,
Welcoming everyone with a waggy tail she meets.
A toy Minion named Bob is her favourite toy,
This goes with her everywhere and brings her joy.

Not very lady-like she does lots of flumps,
On my knee she likes to jump.
Filey Beach is her special place to be,
She absolutely adores walking and paddling in the sea.
Chasing her own tail round and round,
She really is a crazy bonkers little hound.
She is also a bit odd, peculiar and strange,
Though these things I would not change.
Sometimes she thinks she is a unicorn,
Wearing her pink jumper she proudly shows off her horn.
Dancing on her back legs is one of her tricks,
'Shake It Off' by Taylor Swift is her best music mix.
She is adorable, cute, friendly and very funny,
I just love being her mummy!

Esmae Irons (9)
Palterton Primary School, Palterton

D-Dog's Job

He wakes up
Thinking he is a pup.
Ready for some trouble
He hops into his air bubble.
Ready for the day he brushes his teeth,
In his bubble after his meat.
Then he steps out of the door
And stamps on the floor
And says, "Roar!"
To a barn door.
That is how he starts his morning,
Giving everyone a forewarning.
Now moving onto his afternoon,
Before he sees the moon.
D-Dog goes for a stroll,
On his afternoon patrol.
He goes to the shop
And heads to the top
To get a delicious clump of food
Which puts him in a good mood.

After dinner he goes back home
Just after a roam.
He sees the moon
And did you know it was June?
That is the story of D-Dog's job,
All in the space of a minute.

Angel Asher (11)
Palterton Primary School, Palterton

Nasty Neckaladon

The neckaladon is vicious and ambitious,
It is illegal to eat but this beast is nutritious.
He lives in the Gulf of Mexico, in the sea,
It's very cool and he won't disagree.
You can train him as much as you want,
But he's aggressive.
Neckaladon is an impressive creature,
When you see his brilliant features.
His fin is a dazzling prong,
Big as a throng.
He dives out of the sea
And goes... "Tee di lee!"
The animal's neck is toweringly tall.
He looks for some cheese
As long as it will freeze.
He zooms across the sea in a breeze
Wanting to be followed by some bees.
That's all about my neckaladon!

Jacob Smith (11)
Palterton Primary School, Palterton

Vulture-ON Takes Flight

Vulture-ON flies in this poem,
With support,
Bored of being escort,
Every time they put him in a show,
The owners have a row.
Vulture-ON is fed-up with being disliked,
He decides he will have a great haircut,
Now he has braver guts!
Vulture-ON can't fly,
He decides he will get a jetpack.
He will never go back!
Vulture-ON's journey goes for four days,
He tried other ways.
Until...
A human shows up, with loving eyes,
She provides him with a gear (flaming red),
A cool haircut
And a cool jetpack.
Now Vulture-ON can fly.

He's loved after all!

Enis Kayran (11)
Palterton Primary School, Palterton

The Queen Called Genie

My dog is a queen
That is never mean.
Roams the hall
But never chases a ball.
Everything about her is amazing and super
Always a blooper.
My perfect puppy
But a little grubby.
I love her so much
And not like my chinchilla
Because she doesn't live in a hutch.
All I know is cuddles
Sometimes when I am in a muddle.
Always my puppy
I have never been so lucky.
To have a pup like you
Even though you try to steal the stew.
I love her so much
So soft to touch.
She took my heart
And is now a part.

Now my world
And she made me twirl.

Niamh Gotteri (10)
Palterton Primary School, Palterton

The Not Normal Cocker Spaniel

This is not just a normal Cocker Spaniel puppy,
This is a crazy and silly puppy for sure.
It even loves going into a field full of balls.
It would like to stay with us when we are eating boars.
We all love our puppy, she is very cute,
It even likes seeing us dig up roots.
The roots are very big when we get them out of the soil,
She loves it every time.
It even knows its two times tables.
It loves going into old stables.
The stables are very rusty
Because it is made out of metal and it rains.
The puppy loves it when it starts raining and hailing,
It starts jumping up and down.

Darcie Bailey (9)
Palterton Primary School, Palterton

Stanley's Moon Mission

Stanley woke, he's just a pup.
Stanley walks to launch platform three gears up.
Stanley boards the Apollo 13 and prepares.
Stanley finally, after 365 days, gets off at the moon.
Stanley finds a space rock.
Sadly the rocket call isn't working
So he makes a makeshift one and calls in a rocket.
So Stanley, Ollie, Luna and Reggie go home together.
Stanley gets given treats by Ollie.
Stanley and Ollie play and live happily ever after.
Stanley goes on a long walk with Ted.
Stanley and Ollie enjoy their day.

Ted Grainger-Grimes (10)
Palterton Primary School, Palterton

The First Dog On The Moon Or Is It?

My dog's name is Poky,
He used to be called Floky.
Round the house he roams,
Searching for a new home.
I think my dog should be an astronaut
Trying to fetch a bone,
No actually, then he would be alone.
At the start he would be excited
Then no longer united.
I don't want that to happen,
I can't imagine.
Life without my Poky Woky.
So if he goes up to space,
Let's turn up the pace
And explore galaxies and the cosmos together,
I hope we're together forever.

Sophie Ford (9)
Palterton Primary School, Palterton

Rosie The Pawsome Pug

Rosie is a beautiful strange pug.
Rosie is a charming, bizarre, adorable dog.
Rosie is an illuminated dog that turns a frown upside down.
Rosie is a loud thing that's louder than a giant's footsteps.
Rosie is a lightning bolt when she runs.
Rosie is a hoover when food gets dropped on the floor.
Rosie is a pug that is 100 times louder than a volcanic eruption.
Rosie is a loving dog that loves protracted walks and sleeps.
That's why Rosie is a pawsome pug.

Harry Carr (11)
Palterton Primary School, Palterton

Meg-O-Night And Barney

You do not want to mess with me.
You will bow down like the rest.
You are the worst, I am the best.
My friend is Barney,
I will stand by him until the end.
Fighting together and ruling the world.
I will never betray him.
We rule, you drool.
He is strong.
He likes to hear a Chinese gong.
He wishes he had more friends.
He is vicious.
He loves tuna.
He's tall and brave.
But if you get to know him
He is great and he is my mate.

Max Slater (11)
Palterton Primary School, Palterton

The Magma

Magma the mat is a big hairy dog
That lives under a rock and has a pet frog.
He begs for walks and steals forks.
He loves a porch to watch children go by.
Magma has a nickname which is Mat.
He wears a fluffy hat and has a bat.
He likes watching football with me and my friends.
When it ends he squeals, wanting it back.
When the TV turns black he runs back and has a snack.
He gets in bed at 4pm and falls into a deep sleep.

Jacob Galley (11)
Palterton Primary School, Palterton

Barnasus' Goal

B arnasus is a good dino with purple skin and
A very, very green belly.
R ufus is a mega knight, Barney's best friend.
N ever stabbing his back until the end.
A nd they will stand side-by-side for days on end.
S o let them fly into the sunset and bring
U tter justice to the world!
S o you can sleep feeling safe at night.

Taylor Kirby (11)
Palterton Primary School, Palterton

My Dough Dough (Dougie)

Dougie is a helpful dog and always full of energy.
Dougie is a doctor, he always knows what to do.
Dougie is a cure for sadness.
Dougie is a rainbow, always puts a smile on your face.
Dougie is a star that can't be missed.
Dougie is a flower, bright as can be.
Dougie is an art picture, colourful like artwork.
Dougie is a perfect (animal) best friend.

Paige Darby (10)
Palterton Primary School, Palterton

The Dino-Dog Discovered

The dino-dog is a rare beast.
The dino-dog is a frightening pet.
The dino-dog is a magnificent beast and guard.
The dino-dog is a hero.
The dino-dog is a protective part dino and part dog.
The dino-dog is an awesome thing to have.
The dino-dog is a lovely wanted dino and dog.
The dino-dog is the bestest pet in the whole wide world!

Troy Everitt (10)
Palterton Primary School, Palterton

Prince Of The Sea

Squidly the ultra-rare squid
Is the ocean's coolest kid!
His best friend is an octopus called Cooper,
Purple and black he looks super duper!
Swimming backwards is his best skill,
He enjoys wearing a dress with a frill.
Diving deep with his tentacles that suck
Whilst reading Harry Potter, his fave book.

Amelia Wombwell (10)
Palterton Primary School, Palterton

Emily, My Unicorn Owl

Emily, my unicorn owl, is a loving owl.
If she ever gets wet she shakes her feathers,
No need for a towel.
Her horn shines bright, especially in the light
And she always shines bright.
Emily, my unicorn owl, thinks she is a unicorn
But I don't tell her
So I'd rather just pet her.

Dacey Harris (9)
Palterton Primary School, Palterton

Benjamin The Lamb

Benjamin the lamb is as beautiful as a puppy.
He is very strong but sometimes a bit shy.
He always makes me smile when I see his cute face.
When I get him milk I always see a smile on his face.
His fur is as fluffy as a pillow.

Archie Clayton (11)
Palterton Primary School, Palterton

My Lamb, Bessie

Bessie is white all over.
She always jumps up at the gate.
This is because she wants her milk.
I see her before I go off to school.
She plays in the barn and the field.
Boomer and Benjamin are her best friends.

Barney Clayton (7)
Palterton Primary School, Palterton

Elvis Wears The Crown

Elvis is my sausage dog
Who makes me laugh all day.
I tell my Elvis to sit
But all Elvis can do is stay.
My snake Steve appears
But Elvis cries with tears.

Jensen Wombwell (10)
Palterton Primary School, Palterton

My Cat, Pip

She's cute and sassy,
I'd say very classy,
Trots with her tail in the air,
You wouldn't want her glare!

Like butter wouldn't melt,
Her name back and forth is the same spelt,
She's the queen of the house,
She's too posh to bring back a mouse!

Massage her face day and night,
Even her chin where it's so white,
Stroke her and love her if you dare,
It's on her terms, as she doesn't care!

Hiba Junaid (10)
Parkinson Lane Community Primary School, Halifax

My Nutty Squirrel

S quirrel makes me nutty.
Q uiet like a thief, he searches for food.
U nlike others, he is very forgetful, where he last dug.
I ntelligent he may think he is yet he loses his food to the thieves.
R odent, sharp teeth, never rests day and night.
R aring to go, he races to his food.
E ach time he hopes he will be the winner.
L onely, he lives in the trees and comes to visit me when I'm free.

Aamnah Javed (10)
Parkinson Lane Community Primary School, Halifax

My Clever Cat, Claire

Claire is my cute cat
Who likes to wear a colourful hat.
She can read and write
But she can't bite.

My cat is very clever,
The most intelligent thing ever.
Claire has a small brain
Which makes her go through pain.

Claire is very good at art
And always tries to take part.
She can even hold a felt tip,
Whilst doing a fantastic flip.

Aleena Ali (10)
Parkinson Lane Community Primary School, Halifax

Rolo

I have a dog called Rolo.
He has a mouth shaped like a Polo.
Both his ears flop
Like my mum's mop.
His tail is puffy,
His coat is so fluffy.
He has a nose as black as coal,
If he sees a muddy puddle he will have a roll.
He is perfect for a cuddle,
We both love to snuggle.
Rolo is like my teddy bear.

Lola Rykala (8)
Turners Hill CE Primary School, Turners Hill

Bodhi, My Pet

B odhi is lazy and sometimes crazy.
O h I love him so
D ashing, daring, loving and caring
H e is tame but for bad smells he is to blame
I love him and he loves me!

Isabelle Violet Staples (8)
Turners Hill CE Primary School, Turners Hill

Leopard Sparkle

I'm a leopard
Spotted with fur.
Don't come near
Or I might grrr!
Don't come near
Or I might miaow!
Don't come near
Or I might growl!

Jessica Thrower (7)
Turners Hill CE Primary School, Turners Hill

Griffintig

Look at the fierce, brave Griffintig
Gnawing on a bone.
How I wish he'd eat a proper dish
And leave my foot alone!

Oliver Thrower (7)
Turners Hill CE Primary School, Turners Hill

I Wish I Had A Bunny

I wish I had a bunny,
I hope she would be very sunny.
I would call her Strawberry,
It would make me merry.
I think she would be so cute,
And I will feed her fruit.
I would brush her fluffy tail,
But she might scratch me with her sharp nails.
I think it is funny,
That I wish I had a bunny.

Jessica Botham (8)
Weston Junior Academy, Weston Coyney

My Nabit Called Charlie

A nabit is a rabbit that nibbles a lot
And eats lots of carrots out of his pot.
My nabit called Charlie is totally gnarly.
My nabit is the best but he can be a pest.
He is a cute bunny who is always eating honey.
I can't pretend that this is the end.

Leon Scholtz (10)
Weston Junior Academy, Weston Coyney

I Wish I Had Some Kittens

I wish I had some kittens,
That I could give some mittens.
My kittens love to play,
On a sunny day.
My kittens would come in at night,
Otherwise they would bite.
I give them their bread
And send them to bed.

Jasmine Dawkins (10)
Weston Junior Academy, Weston Coyney

The Confused Jellyfish

The confused jellyfish, on the land
He tries to walk
He thinks he's a man.

The confused jellyfish wasn't ordinary
It was grumpy in water
And quite a smelly fish
The jellyfish was quite extraordinary.

People say it's rather dangerous
For me it's rather not
To be stung by a jellyfish is quite hazardous
And makes your legs go hot, hot, hot.

The confused jellyfish likes land
Not quite the sea
Maybe it's just the sand?
If you listen when he is out and about
It makes him laugh and shout with glee.

The confused jellyfish is now trying to walk
Don't go to the beach
Or you might get caught.

Angel Reid-Holden (11)
Winterbourne Boys' Academy, Thornton Heath

My Peculiar Pet

My pet is unique,
It can fly up to a mountain peak,
My pet is called a dracocat,
And instead of catching mice, it catches rats,
Dracocats are extremely rare,
So you have to look after them with care.

I named my pet Drake,
But I think that was a mistake,
Because when I say I'm going to get my pet,
People hear Drake then they get upset,
Because I tell them Drake is my pet.

Drake can breathe fire,
And is so clever it can put on work attire,
Although the clothing never fits
Mostly because Drake burns it to bits,
Oh, and did I mention Drake is a he,
Just like me?

Raza Khan (11)
Winterbourne Boys' Academy, Thornton Heath

My Dog Is Loyal

I have a dog named Zeus,
He is very loyal
Because we give him love, food and shelter.
When I go to school he is very quiet,
Must be missing me, same as I do
So, when he sees me coming back from school
He goes crazy again.
He likes to play with me
But I have to do my homework.
My mum and Mr Southgate are very strict
So I have little time to play with Zeus in the week.
At the weekends I take him walking in the park.
Zeus likes his balls and cosy bed,
Soft pillow and all my toys.
He is very clever.
I am so proud of my dog.
He is adorable and cute.
I like Zeus very much.

Dhyan Patel (9)
Winterbourne Boys' Academy, Thornton Heath

Legendary The Sabretooth

There was a sabretooth
That was like the tiger
But one day a tiger came to challenge him
But Legendary was always ready.
When he found out that it was 10 vs 1
He couldn't afford to let his guard down,
For one of the tigers to beat him
So instead he went on a rage
And took out the tigers one by one
Till there was one last tiger standing.
Suddenly they had a furious fight
To see who would win
But one of Legendary's legs was hurting
He couldn't bear to lose but at the same time
He was about to let his guard down.

Richard Agyei Opoku (10)
Winterbourne Boys' Academy, Thornton Heath

Cat Playing Cricket

The cat came out to play,
However, there was a delay
As the cat had not a bat to play the game,
So he decided to bowl to practise his aim.
As he bowled the ball
It flew like a cannonball,
Heading straight towards the wicket,
This could be his career ticket.
As the ball hit the stumps, the crowd jumped.
The cat fell to the floor and landed with a thump,
The batsman was out without a doubt.
There you have it, a cat playing cricket,
And made his first wicket!

Nathaniel Suthaskumar (10)
Winterbourne Boys' Academy, Thornton Heath

Ocean Is Annoying

Ocean is annoying and fat
Because he loves eating rats
And vomits on the mat.
He always eats my hats.
Mum says he is lazy
But I think he's amazing.
He plays with the yarn
And scares the cows in the barn.
I'm sure he means no harm.
Never mind he just bit my arm.
Ocean is annoying,
That is why I am writing this poem.

Hamed Jimoh (11)
Winterbourne Boys' Academy, Thornton Heath

Fish In A Dish

Fish might live on a dish
But fish can only swim in a tank.
Salmon fish live in a lake
Which is bigger than a cake.

I found my Nemo at the pet shop
Because I liked his flip and flop.
We took him home.
I fed Nemo,
He grew stronger and faster.

Reuben Oviawe (7)
Winterbourne Boys' Academy, Thornton Heath

YOUNG WRITERS INFORMATION

We hope you have enjoyed reading this book – and that you will continue to in the coming years.

If you're a young writer who enjoys reading and creative writing, or the parent of an enthusiastic poet or story writer, visit our website www.youngwriters.co.uk/subscribe to join the World of Young Writers and receive news, competitions, writing challenges, tips, articles and giveaways! There is lots to keep budding writers motivated to write!

If you would like to order further copies of this book, or any of our other titles, then please give us a call or order via your online account.

Young Writers
Remus House
Coltsfoot Drive
Peterborough
PE2 9BF
(01733) 890066
info@youngwriters.co.uk

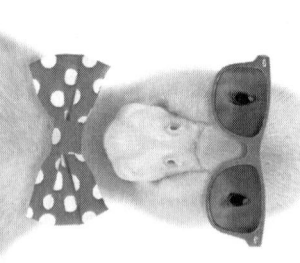

Join in the conversation!
Tips, news, giveaways and much more!

 YoungWritersUK    YoungWritersCW    youngwriterscw